To Rachel Cole and Michael Etkin

The
After School
Book

Written by Stephanie Calmenson
Illustrated by Beth Lee Weiner

Publishers · GROSSET & DUNLAP · New York

CONTENTS

A Rainy Afternoon

Every day after school, Mrs. Owl waited to walk
Owlet home.

"See you tomorrow!" called Owlet to his friends.

"How was school today?" asked Mrs. Owl.

"It was fun. We read a story about a train that couldn't get up a mountain and then did. And we fingerpainted. See?"

"Yes, I do see," said Mrs. Owl. "There is a little paint on the paper and a lot of paint on you!"

"Which picture do you like better, Mommy?" Owlet laughed.

At home, Owlet's mother hung up his painting
and then helped him take off his shirt.

"Would you play with me, Mommy?" Owlet
asked.

"I'd like to," said Owlet's mother, "but I have the
laundry to do. Why don't you play with your toys?"

9

Owlet wandered into his room. He took his fire truck out of the toy chest. Ding, ding! Ding, ding!

Owlet raced around the room and stopped in front of his play house. He waved the hose at the make-believe fire.

"Whoosh! I put that fire out fast," he said.

Next, Owlet piled up his building blocks one by one until he could hardly reach the top.

He knew that one more block would make the tower fall. But he stretched way up and put the last one on anyway. Sure enough, the tower came crashing down.

"Are you all right, Owlet?" called his mother.

"Yes, Mommy," he answered.

Owlet was lonely. He liked playing by himself sometimes. But today he wanted company.

He looked out the window and saw that it had started to rain. Inside the room was warm, but outside it was cool. So the window started to get steamy.

Owlet liked when that happened. He could make pictures with his wing on the foggy glass.

In the places where Owlet drew, he was able to
see out the window again. He saw a garbage truck
drive by. When it passed, he saw Mrs. Muskrat
mailing a letter.

"She's all alone, too," thought Owlet.

13

"Mommy!" Owlet called, running to find her.
"Can we ask Mrs. Muskrat over to play?"

"That's a good idea, Owlet. I've been meaning to
call her."

Together, Owlet and his mother called Mrs.
Muskrat. She said she would be delighted to come.

"I'll put up water for tea and cocoa, and we can make toast," said Mrs. Owl. "Will you set the table?"

Owlet went right to work. "We'll need one... two... three of everything," he counted.

Owlet was so excited about having company that he started to sing:

I'm a little teapot, short and stout.
Here is my handle, here is my spout.
When I get all steamed up, hear me shout.
Tip me over and pour me out!

The kettle started to whistle, and soon the toast popped up. Mrs. Owl cut the toast into triangles. Owlet put a pat of butter on each one and sprinkled cinnamon on top. They were ready for their guest.

17

Mrs. Muskrat arrived with some daisies from her
garden and a bag of tiny white marshmallows for
the cocoa.

"Thank you for inviting me," she said.

"We're glad you could come," said Mrs. Owl.

Owlet showed Mrs. Muskrat his painting and taught her the teapot song. And together they talked and laughed away the rainy afternoon.

Show and Tell

Porcupine's mother used to meet her after school. Then she had to go to work. So Porcupine spent the afternoons with Mrs. Badger, her babysitter.

"Are you ready to feed the ducks?" asked Mrs. Badger.

"I'm ready!" said Porcupine.

"Do you have any homework?" Mrs. Badger asked.

"I need something for *Show and Tell* tomorrow," Porcupine answered.

"Maybe you'll find something at the pond," Mrs. Badger said.

They could already hear the ducks quacking. Porcupine ran ahead and threw some bread to them. But it was windy and the bread didn't go very far. Only one brave duckling came up from the water.

"Look," said Porcupine, "he isn't afraid at all."

Porcupine stood still so she wouldn't frighten the duckling. She whispered to him, "Tomorrow is *Show and Tell.* Would you come to school with me?"

The duckling didn't answer. He just finished his meal and hurried back to the water.

Porcupine threw up her arms.
"Silly duck!" she called.
Just then Porcupine saw something move. It was
something big and dark. She tiptoed toward it. It
moved away. She waved her arms again. It waved
its arms, too.

"You've found your shadow!" called
Mrs. Badger.

"Can I bring it to *Show and Tell*?" asked
Porcupine.

She ran after her shadow but couldn't catch it.
Porcupine was disappointed.

"Come," said Mrs. Badger. "I have an idea."

At her house, Mrs. Badger hung a big piece of
paper on the wall. Then she shined a bright light
on Porcupine and began to draw Porcupine's
shadow. When Mrs. Badger got to her toes,
Porcupine started to laugh.

"That tickles!" she said.

"You're so silly," said Mrs. Badger, smiling.

Porcupine's mother came to get her right on
time.

"I like your shadow," she said. They rolled it up
carefully so Porcupine could take it to school.

"See you tomorrow," called Porcupine to
Mrs. Badger.

The next day at *Show and Tell*, Porcupine
unrolled her drawing. She told the class all about
her afternoon at the pond.

"And this is what my shadow looked like. I
waved my arms, and it waved its arms, too. I ran
after it, but I couldn't catch it," she explained.

27

When she was finished, the class clapped. Porcupine took a bow. Right behind her, her shadow bowed, too.

Rabbit Remembers

Rabbit and Bear were on their way to The Mulberry Arts and Crafts Center.

"There is something I forgot to do in school today," said Rabbit to Bear.

"What did you forget?" Bear asked.

"I don't know because I forgot it," answered Rabbit.

29

At the Center, Mrs. Otter greeted the children.

"Hello, Rabbit. What would you like to do today?"

"I'm going to cut and paste with Bear," said Rabbit.

"Why don't you use these shapes?" Mrs. Otter suggested. "Can you help me name them?" she asked.

Rabbit and Bear named the circles, triangles, and squares.

"At least I remembered that," thought Rabbit.

"Have fun," said Mrs. Otter.

While they worked, Rabbit and Bear talked about their day at school.

"I wish Beaver wouldn't push me on the milk and cookie line," Bear said.

"You should tell him not to," Rabbit said, snipping out a square.

Rabbit pasted down the square and began singing to himself, *"Happy Birthday to you, Happy Birthday to you…"*

"Why are you singing that?" asked Bear.

Rabbit looked up. "That's it!" he shouted. "That's what I forgot! It's Grandpa's birthday, and I was going to make a present for him." Rabbit started to cry.

"It's all right," said Mrs. Otter. "You remembered in time."

She took the paper with the shapes pasted on it and folded it in half.

"You can give him this beautiful card."

Then Mrs. Otter took out some paper
and drew a red shape.
"That's a heart!" said Rabbit.
And he cut it out to paste inside.

"What would you like to say, Rabbit?" asked Mrs. Otter.

"Happy Birthday, Grandpa. I love you."

Mrs. Otter wrote Rabbit's message, and then Rabbit wrote his name.

"Can I write my name, too?" asked Bear.

"And me?" asked Squirrel, Chipmunk, and Mole.

Soon everyone had signed the card.

When Rabbit's Grandpa came to pick him up,
Rabbit gave him the card.

"My birthday!" Grandpa said. "I knew I forgot
something! Thank you, Rabbit."

Rabbit hugged his Grandpa. He was glad he
had remembered.

The Popcorn Party

It was Raccoon's turn to have the playgroup at his house.

"Hold on tight, everybody," said Mr. Raccoon.

Raccoon, Beaver, and Groundhog were talking about the party in school that day.

"I wish it was somebody's birthday every day!" said Raccoon.

"I wish it was *my* birthday every day," said Groundhog.

"But then you would get old so fast," Beaver told him.

Only Skunk was quiet. She was tired. "Noisy party, noisy wagon," she thought.

As soon as they got to Raccoon's house, Beaver
ran to the bathroom. Raccoon and Groundhog
went to the toy chest. Then Mr. Raccoon came
into the room and looked around.

"Where is Skunk?" he asked.

"She's not here," said Groundhog and Raccoon.

"And she's not in the bathroom, either," said
Beaver, who was just returning.

Mr. Raccoon went to look for Skunk. He found
her sitting in the wagon outside.

"What's the matter, Skunk? Did somebody hurt
your feelings?"

"I just want to be by myself," Skunk said.

"Come inside," said Mr. Raccoon. "We'll show
you what Raccoon does whenever he wants
to be alone."

"Watch this!" said Raccoon. He made a castle
of four chairs and a blanket.

"Come out as soon as you're ready," said
Mr. Raccoon.

"Goodbye," said Groundhog.

"We'll miss you," said Beaver.

Skunk took a book and a flashlight and
disappeared beneath the blanket.

The three friends went back to playing, but not
for long.

"I'm hungry," said Groundhog.

"Let's have some popcorn!" said Raccoon.

And he went to ask his father if it was all right
to make some.

Mr. Raccoon spread a sheet in the middle of the floor and put the popcorn machine on it.

They each took turns pouring in the corn. Then Mr. Raccoon taped a long string onto the floor.

"No one is allowed to cross this line," he said. "I don't want anyone to get hurt."

Mr. Raccoon turned on the machine, and the corn started popping.

Raccoon, Beaver, and Groundhog sang:

> *Pop! Pop!*
> *Pop! Pop! Pop!*
> *Pop! Pop!*
> *Do the popcorn hop!*

They were all careful not to cross the line. And
the corn kept popping.

Finally it stopped. But a voice from the castle
kept singing:

Pop! Pop!
Pop! Pop! Pop!

Raccoon lifted the blanket and Skunk popped
out.

"I'm finished being alone," she said.

And Skunk hopped to the line to join the
popcorn party.